GEOGRAPHY *for fun*

Food and Farming

Pam Robson

Copper Beech Books
Brookfield, Connecticut

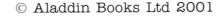

Produced by
Aladdin Books Ltd
28 Percy Street
London W1P 0LD

First published in the United States
in 2001 by
Copper Beech Books,
an imprint of
The Millbrook Press
2 Old New Milford Road
Brookfield, Connecticut 06804

Editor: Kathy Gemmell

Designer: Simon Morse

Illustrator: Tony Kenyon

Picture researcher: Brian Hunter Smart

Printed in UAE

Library of Congress Cataloging-in-Publication Data

Robson, Pam.
Food and farming / Pam Robson ; [illustrator, Tony Kenyon].
p. cm. -- (Geography for fun)
ISBN 0-7613-2424-0 (lib.bdg.)
1. Agriculture--Experiments--Juvenile literature. 2.
Food--Experiments--Juvenile literature. [1. Agriculture--Experiments. 2.
Food--Experiments. 3. Experiments.] I. Kenyon, Tony, ill. II. Title.
S519 .R68 2001
630'.78--dc21
2001028819

The author, Pam Robson, is an experienced teacher.
She has written and advised on many books for children
on geography and science subjects.

CONTENTS

INTRODUCTION

Geography is about people and places and all the changes that take place in the world. Once, people had to hunt for food. Then people learned how to collect and grow grass seed and to herd animals. Farming had begun. Now, the population of the world is growing fast, so more and more food is needed. Some farmers are changing their methods so that they can produce more crops. Learning about where food comes from will help you understand the importance of farming all over the world.

1 Look for numbers like this. Each step for the projects inside the book has been numbered this way. To draw the maps and make the models shown in each project, make sure that you follow the steps in the right order.

FEATURE BOXES
● Look for the feature boxes on each double page. They either give further information about the project on the page, or they suggest other fun activities for you to do. Remember, geography is all around you. Use the ideas in this book to help you think up some geography projects of your own.

WHAT'S HAPPENING

● The What's Happening paragraphs explain the geography behind the projects you do or make.

● The Helpful Hints on some pages give you tips for doing the projects.

● Look at the Glossary at the back of this book to find out what important words mean.

● Always use the most up-to-date maps, atlases, websites, and reference books.

● Use the atlas index to find the location of any place you are looking for.

WARNING

● This sign means that you must take extra care when doing the project. Always tell an adult where you are going and what you are doing. Ask an adult to help if you need to use a sharp tool. Be especially careful when you are out collecting information in the countryside —always follow paths and close any gates. Make sure you wash your hands after handling soil or moldy food.

POPULATION AND FOOD

In 1999, the population of the world reached 6 billion. Every person needs food to survive, so food supply has to increase as the number of people increases. The supply of food depends mainly on farmers. However, only certain parts of the Earth's surface are suitable for farming. Countries with the most people to feed—in parts of Africa, South America, and Asia—are also among the poorest areas of the world. Here, many farmers can produce only enough food for their own families.

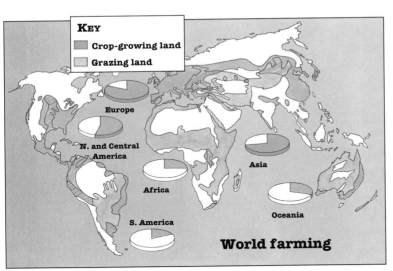

KEY
Crop-growing land
Grazing land

Europe

N. and Central America

Africa

Asia

S. America

Oceania

World farming

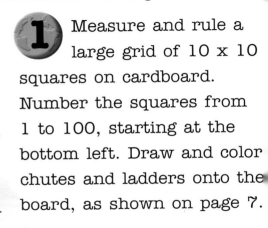

This map and the pie charts show roughly how much land in each continent is used for productive crop farming. Grassland areas are used for grazing livestock. The white areas are not used or are not suitable for farming.

UPS AND DOWNS OF FARMING

Farmers need good weather and rich soil or their crops will fail. Crops are also destroyed by disease and natural disasters. Make a game to show the ups and downs of farming.

1 Measure and rule a large grid of 10 x 10 squares on cardboard. Number the squares from 1 to 100, starting at the bottom left. Draw and color chutes and ladders onto the board, as shown on page 7.

2 Now use the key to help you design and draw symbols showing farming "ups"—things that help a food crop—and "downs"—things that destroy a food crop. Draw a "down" symbol at the top of each chute, and an "up" symbol at the bottom of each ladder.

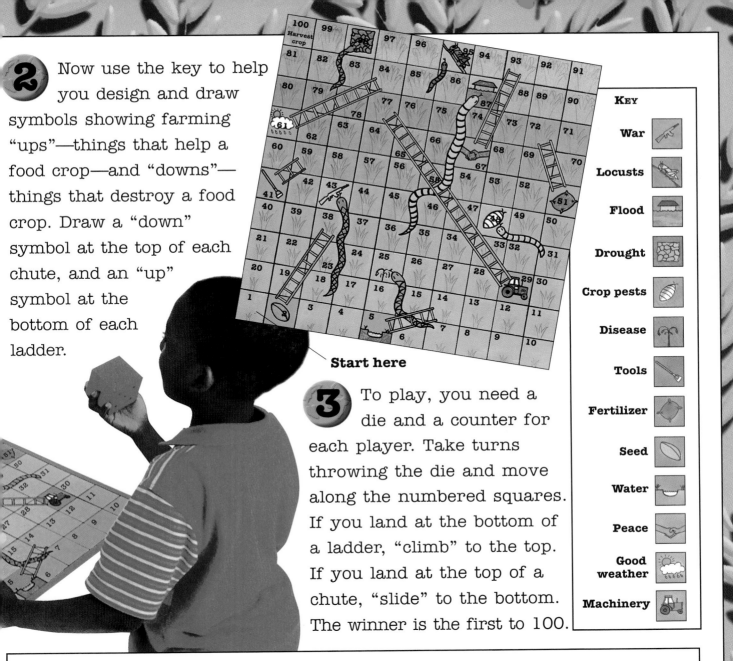

Start here

3 To play, you need a die and a counter for each player. Take turns throwing the die and move along the numbered squares. If you land at the bottom of a ladder, "climb" to the top. If you land at the top of a chute, "slide" to the bottom. The winner is the first to 100.

KEY

War	
Locusts	
Flood	
Drought	
Crop pests	
Disease	
Tools	
Fertilizer	
Seed	
Water	
Peace	
Good weather	
Machinery	

STAPLE DIETS
● The food crop that grows best and is eaten most in any one country is called its staple diet. Most staple diets are cereal crops, like wheat. In developed countries, where food is plentiful, some people eat a staple diet of fast food, such as burgers.

Wheat, grown in temperate regions, is used to make bread and pasta.

Rice is the staple diet in many developing countries.

Maize, or corn, is the staple diet in parts of Africa and S. America. In the U.S., it is used mainly to feed livestock.

ALL YEAR ROUND

All farmers must prepare the soil, fertilize, plow, sow seed, nurture (look after), and harvest their crops. When these tasks are done depends upon climate and weather. In temperate climates, which are neither too hot nor too cold, farmers rely on the right kind of weather for each season. In spring, when seeds are sown, they hope for sunshine and showers. At harvest time, in late summer, they hope for dry weather with lots of sunshine. Farmers in the developed world use machinery to plant and harvest in large fields.

Plowing
A plow is a farm tool that turns over and breaks up the soil before seed is planted in the spring. Modern plows, such as the moldboard (left), are pulled by a tractor. They have metal blades that cut into the soil.

Sowing
In many developing countries, seed is still sown by hand. In developed countries, farmers use mechanical planters, or seed drills, pulled by tractors.

Growing and harvesting
Crops need rich soil, sunshine, and moisture to grow well. When they are ripe, the crops can be harvested quickly by combine harvesters. These machines combine the cutting and threshing (sorting grain from straw).

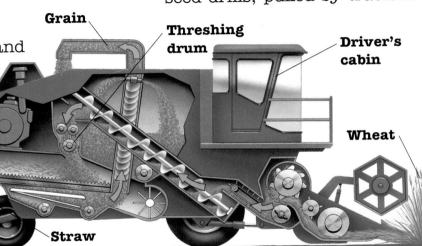

Grain

Threshing drum

Driver's cabin

Wheat

Straw

CLOUD-WATCHER

Clouds are made up of tiny water droplets. Rain falls when the droplets become too big. Farmers use clouds to forecast the weather. Make a chart to record the daily weather where you are.

Weather chart		
Date	Temp.	Cloud & rain
March 5th	50°F	rain all day
March 6th	48°F	drizzle
March 7th	51°F	no rain
arch 8th	50°F	heavy rain
rch 9th	55°F	clear sky, no rain
ch th	53°F	no rain
h h	55°F	no rain

HELPFUL HINTS

● How many sayings about weather do you know? Keep a record to see if the ones you know are true or not.

1 Record the clouds each day for a week. What do they look like? Is any rain falling from them? Is the rain a drizzle or a downpour?

Cirrus clouds are high and wispy. Cirrus means "curl of hair."

Stratus clouds form a low, gray blanket. Stratus means "layer."

Cumulus clouds are either small and fluffy, or they tower into tall, billowing storm clouds. Cumulus means "heap."

2 Note the temperature each day. Place a thermometer outdoors, out of direct sunlight. Always take your readings at the same time each day.

SOIL

● When wind and rain erode (wear away) rock, they break it down into rock particles. These particles mix with humus to form soil. Humus is the decomposed (rotted) bodies of dead plants and animals. It binds the soil particles together and holds moisture.

Humus is found in topsoil and is rich in nutrients (goodness). Crops need nutrients to grow. Minibeasts like worms live here.

Subsoil contains more rock particles than humus. In rich soil, rainwater and roots should be able to reach into the subsoil.

Broken rocks lie between the subsoil and the bedrock. Groundwater can only seep as far as the bedrock. Very few roots reach here.

PRODUCING FOOD

The kind of farming practiced in temperate regions depends upon soil type and the condition of the land. Arable farming (the growing of crops) is done on low-lying land where the soil is rich. Sheep farming is done in hilly regions. Dairy farming is done on low-lying, rich grassland. Raising animals for food is called livestock farming. Poultry farmers raise birds, like chickens, for food. Mixed farming combines growing crops and raising animals. Truck farmers grow fruits and vegetables for sale in nearby cities.

FARMINOES

Learn about farms by playing "farminoes." You will need paper, cardboard, glue, scissors, and colored pencils.

1 Draw 28 domino shapes onto paper, then copy the farminoes shown below.

Arable farm	Arable farm	Arable farm	Arable farm	Barley	Tractor	Harvester	Sheep farm	Sheep farm	Sheep
Cow	Mixed farm	Wheat	Apple	Poultry farm	Sheep farm	Pig farm	Milking machine	Mixed farm	Pig farm
Truck farm	Truck farm	Truck farm	Mixed farm	Potato	Carrot	Dairy farm	Pig	Pig farm	Dairy farm
Mixed farm	Lamb	Pig	Pear	Dairy farm	Arable farm	Piglets	Mixed farm	Piglets	Cows
Poultry farm	Poultry farm	Poultry farm	Turkey	Goose	Milk	Sheep farm	Mixed farm		
Duck	Sheep	Mixed farm	Pig farm	Dairy farm	Mixed farm	Sheep dog	Mixed farm		

Any crop or animal can match the Mixed farm cards.

2 Ask an adult to help you glue your farminoes onto cardboard, then cut them out.

3 Divide the farminoes equally. Up to four people can play. The first player puts down a farmino, picture side up. The next player must match the crop or animal with the farm type, or the farm type with the crop or animal, as shown here. Take turns matching farminoes. If you cannot play, miss a turn. The winner is the first to have no farminoes left.

FACTORY FARMING

● On factory farms, egg-laying hens live side by side in cages with little room to move. Each hen lays more than 200 eggs a year, but many hens become sick and anxious. Some people prefer to buy free-range eggs, which are laid by hens that have more space to move around.

FOOD MOUNTAINS

● In developed countries, many farmers produce more food than they can sell, due to modern machines and intensive farming methods. The surplus (leftover) food is stored in huge "mountains." In developing countries, farmers cannot produce enough food. Many can only grow enough for their own families, so some people starve. Sometimes, the surplus food is used to help emergency food aid programs in areas where people are starving.

FARM TO TABLE

Farmers work directly with the earth, and are called primary producers. Many farm products, such as eggs, livestock, grains, and vegetables are processed by secondary producers to make other useful things. The products that come from corn (maize) include breakfast cereals and corn syrup, which is used to sweeten soft drinks. Wheat kernels are ground to a fine powder called flour, which is used to make bread. Fruits can be made into juices.

Wheat kernel

Husk
Bran
Germ

White flour is made from the soft insides of the kernel.

FARMING PAIRS

Pair up farm crops and farm animals with the products made from them. You will need cardboard, paper, scissors, glue, and colored pencils.

1 Cut out 20 cards from the cardboard. Copy the pictures on the key opposite onto a sheet of paper. Cut each picture out and glue it onto one of your cards. Write the name of each crop or product on the card, as shown. Place the cards upside down in a pile.

2 Two can play. Deal five cards each. Take turns picking a card from the pile. If you can make a pair, lay it in front of you. The first to collect five matching pairs is the winner.

KEY

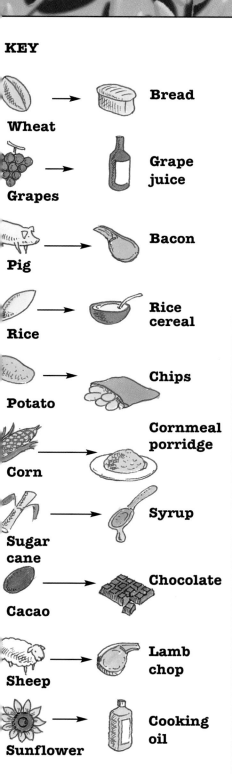

Wheat → Bread

Grapes → Grape juice

Pig → Bacon

Rice → Rice cereal

Potato → Chips

Corn → Cornmeal porridge

Sugar cane → Syrup

Cacao → Chocolate

Sheep → Lamb chop

Sunflower → Cooking oil

You can add more cards to the game by drawing other farm products and the things they are made into.

CATTLE

● Cattle are herbivores, which means they eat plants. They can graze over a large area, finding enough to eat even on poor grazing land. Products that come from cows include leather, milk, beef, and beef fat.

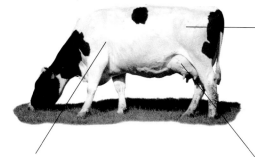

Cow hide is turned into leather for bags, jackets, and shoes.

Milk from dairy cows is made into cheese, yogurt, and butter.

Beef cattle are often sent to feed lots, where they can be fattened quickly before being butchered. They are fed concentrated food for quick growth.

Beef fat is used in cooking and is added to processed foods.

● Livestock can suffer from various diseases. In parts of Africa, the tsetse fly carries a parasite that feeds on the blood of cattle. BSE, or "mad cow disease," spread through several European countries in the 1990s. Thousands of cows were slaughtered (killed), and some people who ate infected meat died. Foot-and-mouth is a highly infectious disease that affects livestock, but is not dangerous to humans. In 1967 and 2001, there were outbreaks in Europe. Thousands of sheep and cattle were slaughtered and burned.

SUSTAINABLE FARMING

Farmers must be able to produce crops year after year. To do this, the soil must remain healthy and fertile. This is called sustainable farming. Modern farming methods and machinery have greatly increased the world's food supply, necessary to feed the growing population. Chemical pesticides and fertilizers are used to produce as many crops as possible. Farmers must make sure that their methods are sustainable—that the crops they plant and chemicals they

Pesticide

use do not destroy the goodness in the soil. Some prefer organic farming—using natural fertilizers.

MINIBEAST DETECTIVE

Minibeasts play a large role in keeping soil healthy. To see them, you need some soil, a large sieve, a fine sieve, a large jar, a magnifying glass, paper towels, and an adjustable lamp.

1 First, remove any sticks and stones from the soil sample. Return any worms you find to the soil outside. Then strain the sample into a bowl through the large sieve. Make sure you wash your hands after you have touched the soil.

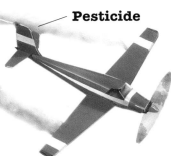

2 Now pour the soil into the fine sieve and balance it above the jar, as shown above. Position the jar beneath the lamp and wait. After a while, you will see some tiny minibeasts appear in the bottom of the jar.

3 Leave the jar for a few hours, then tip the contents onto the paper towels. Examine the minibeasts closely with a magnifying glass. Use a reference book to identify them, then return them to the soil outside.

WHAT'S HAPPENING

● Tiny creatures in soil prefer cool, damp conditions beneath the ground. The heat from the lamp warms the soil, and the minibeasts try to escape from the heat into the jar below. These small creatures are vital to the soil. They help maintain its goodness by breaking down dead matter and adding nutrients.

KEEPING SOIL HEALTHY

● Each crop adds or removes different nutrients from the soil. For example, corn takes nitrogen out of the soil, while crops called legumes—peas or beans—put nitrogen back into the soil. To keep the soil healthy, many farmers change the crops grown in a field from one year to the next. This is called crop rotation.

Field 1:
1st year: Corn
2nd year: Peas
3rd year: Wheat
4th year: Potatoes

Field 2:
1st year: Peas
2nd year: Wheat
3rd year: Potatoes
4th year: Corn

Field 4:
1st year: Potatoes, 2nd year: Corn
3rd year: Peas, 4th year: Wheat

Field 3:
1st year: Wheat, 2nd year: Potatoes
3rd year: Corn, 4th year: Peas

● Some farmers use insects to help keep the soil healthy. Ladybugs eat aphids, which eat crops. Relationships like this exist within every natural food web. Planting onions between crops can also deter pests without having to use chemical pesticides. Many people prefer to eat food that has been grown this way, called organic food.

Aphids

Ladybug

LAND USE

Farming has greatly changed the way land is used. Every farm was once natural countryside. Most farming 100 years ago was done on small farms. Today's arable farms often cover huge areas with a single crop, called a monoculture. This is known as intensive farming. Intensive farming can produce more crops than a small farm can, and the crops or products can be sold more cheaply. Machinery and methods have improved so much that far fewer people need to work on the land. But monocultures have changed the environment, too. Wild animals and plants that adapted to small farms, living in meadows and windbreaks, can't find enough food in monocultures.

WHAT GROWS WHERE?

Make a map to show how land is used for different kinds of farming. You can include small farms and monocultures. You will need paper and some colored pencils.

Wheat

Fruit trees **Poultry**

Soybeans

Cattle

Fruit trees

Corn

Some farmers leave uncultivated areas on the edges of fields for wildlife.

1 Look at the different kinds of farm shown earlier in this book. If there are any farms near your home, think about what kinds of farm they are. What crops are growing? Are there any monocultures? Is there any livestock?

2 Choose which farms you want to show on your map. Draw an outline of fields onto the paper.

3 Color your map and design a key. Use different colors to show the type of farming that is being done in each field. Draw symbols for each of the landmarks or buildings on your map.

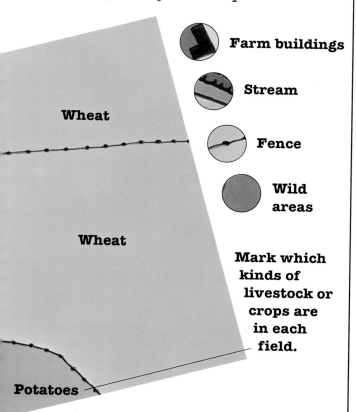

Farm buildings

Stream

Fence

Wild areas

Mark which kinds of livestock or crops are in each field.

Wheat

Wheat

Potatoes

HELPFUL HINTS

● Look at a large-scale map to see if there is any farmland near your house or town. If there is, ask an adult to visit the area with you to look at the kind of farming that is done there.

HABITAT DESTRUCTION

● As natural countryside is plowed up, the wildflowers that grow there are gradually disappearing. The insects that feed on the flowers are going too, which means that birds that feed on the insects are becoming rare. Many songbird species that used to be common on farmland are now endangered.

● Trees and windbreaks help keep the soil in place. Many have been ripped out to make larger fields and, over the years, wind and rain have eroded (worn away) the soil. This has created dustbowls in some areas, where no plants can grow.

● Land around or on farms is often used for recreation. People using the countryside need to follow certain rules to protect the area for farming, wildlife, and for other people to use.

Never leave litter. It can be dangerous for animals.

Keep dogs on a leash so that they do not chase livestock.

TROPICAL FARMING

Many developing countries have tropical climates. In tropical regions, there is a wet season and a dry season, but it is hot all year round. In some places, it is possible to have two harvests in one year. Crops that grow well in tropical climates include coffee, tea, and rice. In the wet season, rainfall is heavy and frequent. On hills, rainwater flows fast down slopes and washes the soil away. This is called soil erosion. Some farmers have learned how to farm slopes by building terraces, like a series of steps.

ON THE TERRACES

To construct your own terraced slope, you will need a deep cardboard box, about 20 inches long and 12 inches wide, a pencil, a craft knife, a trash bag, a plant trough, soil, small stones, and a pitcher of water.

1 Ask an adult to help you cut the cardboard box with the craft knife, so that the sides slope, as shown here. Cut a V-shape in the front. Line the inside of the box with the trash bag.

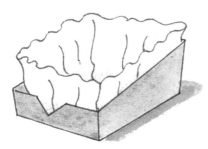

2 Cover the bottom of the lined box with soil. Pile up the soil, so that it is much higher at the back of the box. Position the trough in front, as shown here. Pour water down the slope and watch how easily the soil washes away.

3 Now flatten the soil into flat "steps." Push small stones into the front of each "step," as shown in the photograph. Now pour water down the slope. Note how the soil stays in place instead of washing away.

WHAT'S HAPPENING

● The steps keep the water from flowing too quickly, taking the soil with it. On real terraces, each step is held back by a wall or by plants with strong roots. Ancient Romans planted grapevines and olive trees on terraces. Today, in many parts of Asia, rice is grown on terraced hillsides.

SOIL DEPTH

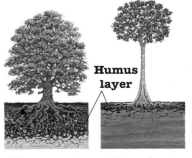

Temperate   Tropical

● In temperate regions, there is usually a deep layer of humus, which contains all the nutrients in the soil. In tropical regions, the nutrients are quickly taken up by plants, which grow well in the hot, moist conditions. Once the nutrients are used up, the humus layer is thin and the soil is no longer any good for growing crops.

SLASH-AND-BURN

Cassava

● Farmers in tropical areas burn trees and bushes to clear ground for planting crops such as cassava. This is called slash-and-burn, or shifting agriculture, because the farmer has to keep on clearing new land. The ashes from the burned wood are full of nutrients, but new crops use up the nutrients quickly. Soon the soil becomes infertile. The farmer then has to start again and burn another area of forest.

NOT ENOUGH FOOD

Although world food production has increased rapidly in the last 50 years, the population has increased even faster. Millions do not have enough to eat and live close to starvation. Millions more are not able to include some important kinds of food in their diet. One big reason for the lack of food is that farmers wear out the soil as they try to produce more and more food from the same land. Natural disasters such as droughts and floods also destroy crops. Many farmers in developing countries do not have the money to buy machinery and tools to improve their farming conditions.

Salt crust

SALTY SOIL

In some areas, the soil can become too salty to grow crops. You can show how this happens in a simple experiment. You will need a tray, soil, salt, and water.

1 Cover the bottom of the tray with about $1/2$ in of salt. Cover the salt with a layer of soil about 2 in deep. Press down firmly.

2 Pour water over the soil and leave the tray in a warm place. Allow the soil to become dry, then water again. Repeat this a few times.

3 Salt crystals will begin to appear on the top of the soil. After about two weeks, a hard crust of salt will form.

WHAT'S HAPPENING

● When there is too much water, the ground becomes waterlogged. In hot sun, surface water evaporates (dries off) quickly and ground water, which contains salts dissolved from rocks, comes up to the surface. This water also evaporates, and the salt left behind forms salt pans. In the Indus valley in Pakistan (left), floods are frequent, and the soil becomes too salty for crops to grow. Each year, there are 100,000 fewer acres to farm.

SUBSISTENCE FARMING

● Farmers who can only grow enough food for their own families are called subsistence farmers. There is a lot of subsistence farming in developing countries. All the planting and harvesting is done by hand. In good years, subsistence farmers may grow enough to sell a few crops at local markets. In drought years, when the rains fail, crops wither, and aid agencies must provide food to prevent the farmers and their families from starving.

Hot, dry winds

Dried-up river

Wilted crops

DROUGHT

● A drought happens when the yearly rains in an area are not heavy enough. Crops and grass for cattle shrivel in the heat. Rivers dry up, and people must walk miles to find water. To help areas that suffer drought frequently, scientists are developing fast-growing seeds that survive on low rainfall.

GLOBAL MARKET

Supermarket shelves hold food crops and products from all over the world. Many are grown in plantations, which are vast monocultures with rows of bushes or trees. Pesticides are used so that as many crops as possible can be produced. In tropical regions, huge plantations of tea (below), sugarcane, pineapples, and coffee are common. In temperate regions, fruit is often grown on plantations. Plantations employ many people to pick and pack the crops.

WHERE DOES IT COME FROM?

Make a map showing where crop products come from. You will need food labels, a map, pencils, cardboard, colored pencils, yarn, pushpins, scissors, and glue.

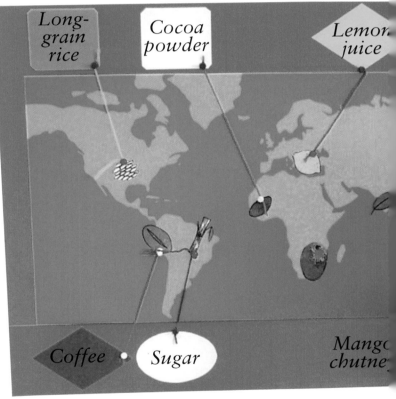

Long-grain rice

Cocoa powder

Lemon juice

Coffee

Sugar

Mango chutney

1 Collect labels from products that come from different countries. Coffee, for example, is grown in Colombia and Kenya. Write down the names of the foods and the names of the countries they come from.

2 Copy a large map of the world. Glue your map onto cardboard, leaving a wide border.

3 Draw and cut out symbols for the food crops you have chosen. Glue the symbols in the correct places on the map. Design and color a key, as shown here.

KEY

Apples   Tea

Sugar   Rice

Cacao   Coffee

Lemons   Mangoes

4 Glue your product labels onto the border. Link each one to the correct food crop on the map using lengths of colored yarn and pushpins.

Tea

CASH CROPS

● Crops grown on plantations in tropical countries and sold all over the world are called cash crops. They are grown especially for export, which means to be sold in other countries. Many countries depend on the money from their cash crops. They suffer greatly if world prices for their crops go down, but gain money to improve farming methods if prices are high.

PLANTATION WORKERS

● Workers employed to cultivate cash crops are often poorly paid, but many prefer the work to subsistence farming. In some countries, a "Fair trade" logo appears on products that come from plantations that pay a decent wage to their workers.

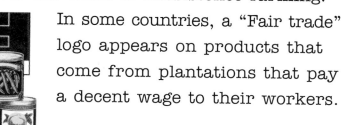

FOOD ON THE MOVE

The banana is a perishable fruit, which means it can rot quickly and lose its value. The banana plant is a huge herb that is so big it is often mistaken for a tree. Huge areas of tropical forest have been cut down so that bananas can be planted as cash crops. Before bananas reach stores, they have a long journey. Look at banana labels to see the many countries in which they are grown. The first bananas grew wild in India. Banana plants were then taken across the world to Central America, where there are now many banana plantations.

1. A stem of bananas can hold 200 bananas, arranged in "hands." Each banana is called a "finger." Workers use a sharp machete, or knife, to cut each stem of green, unripe bananas from the banana plant.

GOING BANANAS

Do an experiment to see how bananas help each other to ripen. You need two unripe bananas, a ripe banana, and two plastic bags.

1 Place one unripe banana in a plastic bag beside the ripe banana. Put the other unripe banana in the second bag.

2 After a few days, compare the bananas. The banana in the bag next to the ripe banana will have ripened faster than the banana in the bag by itself.

WHAT'S HAPPENING

● Bananas naturally produce a gas called ethylene, which makes other bananas ripen. So a ripe banana will make a green banana ripe if they are placed side by side. Just before green bananas reach supermarkets, ethylene gas is used to ripen them quickly.

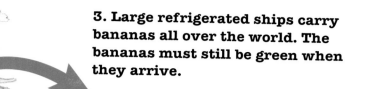

2. The bananas are loaded into rail trucks, or hung on cables, to be transported for packing. They are washed, cut from their stems, and packed in cartons, then taken to be loaded onto ships.

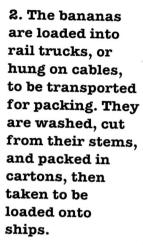

3. Large refrigerated ships carry bananas all over the world. The bananas must still be green when they arrive.

4. Refrigerated trucks meet the ship and swiftly transport the green bananas to supermarket depots.

5. In the supermarket, you can buy fresh bananas all year round.

IMPORTED FOOD

● A long time ago, fruit and vegetables from temperate regions were only on sale after harvest time. Now, shoppers can buy fresh carrots or apples at any time of year. Perishable foods from all over the world are on sale in supermarkets because they can be transported long distances at great speed. Look closely at the labels on fresh fruit and vegetables. Make a note of where they come from, as shown here.

Celery from California

Zucchini from Texas

Chili peppers from Mexico

Grapefruit from Florida

Pears from Oregon

Raspberries from Canada

Apples from South Africa

Cabbage from New York

Mushrooms from Pennsylvania

Asparagus from Michigan

ON THE SHELVES

Much of the food we buy in stores has been preserved in some way. This means that the normal rotting process has been slowed down so that the food stays fresh longer. Without food preservation, food would spoil as it is transported from farms to cities or from country to country. Most people would have to grow their own food. Refrigerating, canning, freezing, pickling, smoking, and drying are all methods of preventing food from spoiling.

MOLDY BREAD

Find out how perishable food, like bread, gets moldy in certain conditions. You will need four slices of white bread and two small plastic bags.

1 Put two slices of bread in separate bags. Place one somewhere cool (in the fridge) and leave the other somewhere warm. Put the other two slices in the same places, but unwrapped.

2 Leave the bread for two days, then observe any changes. The warm slice in the bag will probably show the most mold. Wash your hands after handling the bread—do NOT eat it!

WHAT'S HAPPENING

● The bag keeps the bread moist. Molds are fungi that grow best in warm, moist conditions. However, because the fungi are hardy, molds will also grow, more slowly, in cooler conditions.

PACKS OF PACKAGES

● Study the food on supermarket shelves and make a list of different ways in which food is preserved. Write down which foods are packaged or preserved in each way. For example:

Drying—raisins, milk
Smoking—bacon, fish
Preserving in sugar—jam
Canning—pears, soups
Freezing—meat, fish,
*   vegetables*
Pickling—onions
Chemical additives—cakes,
*   cheese, fruit juices*

● Look closely at the wording on a chips package. What information does the manufacturer provide? See if the same information is provided on all the other packages and cans you found.

NEW IMPROVED FLAVOR!

Best Before: July 07, 2003

Ingredients: dried potato, vegetable oil, potato starch, acidity regulator, flavor, flavor enhancers, citric acid, sweeteners, wheat flour, salt, butter oil.

34g

CHIPS

Nutritional information: (values per 100g) energy-528 kcal protein-3.0g carbohydrates-58.3 g sugars-1.3g fat-31.4g saturates-14.2g fiber-2.0g sodium-1.3g

Fab Foods PO Box No. 4 Willington New York, USA customer care: 0800 848 848 website www.ffffab.com

"Best before" date

Ingredients

Package weight

Manufacturer's details

Nutritional information

WASTE PACKAGING

● Although many foods are packaged to preserve them, some are packaged just to sell them. Packaging material creates mountains of trash that must be disposed of. Most of our trash is buried in the ground in landfill sites. But many landfill sites are now full. The best way to reduce the amount of trash is to use less packaging.

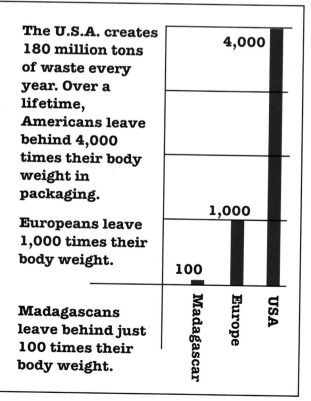

The U.S.A. creates 180 million tons of waste every year. Over a lifetime, Americans leave behind 4,000 times their body weight in packaging.

Europeans leave 1,000 times their body weight.

Madagascans leave behind just 100 times their body weight.

4,000

1,000

100

Madagascar | Europe | USA

HEALTHY EATING

Food provides us with energy. Most people in developed countries are able to gain enough energy to live healthily by eating a balanced diet, which means eating a variety of foods. In developing countries, it is often more difficult to eat a balanced diet, because farmers are not able to produce enough food for everyone. Farmers and scientists are always trying to develop new farming methods and improve seeds so that more food can be grown, especially in poor soil and poor growing conditions.

A balanced diet includes many kinds of food.

The diet in a developing country may include food from only one or two food groups.

FOOD VALUES

● The body needs four main groups of nutrients to stay healthy, as well as minerals and water. The four groups are carbohydrates, proteins, vitamins, and fats.

Carbohydrates are energy-giving starches in foods such as bread and potatoes; and sugars in foods such as cookies.

Proteins, in meat, eggs, and fish, help growth and repair of the body.

Vitamins are needed to maintain good health. Fruit and vegetables are especially high in certain vitamins.

Fats, in butter and meat, also give the body energy.

WEEKLY FOOD INTAKE

Keep a record of the food you eat every day for a week to find out how balanced your diet is. You will need a notebook, a ruler, and a pencil.

1 Use the ruler to draw five columns in your food intake chart. Write headings for the day and time in the first column, then the four food groups: carbohydrates, proteins, vitamins, and fats, in the other columns.

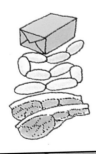

2 Every time you have a meal, make a note of what you eat. Write each piece of food in the correct column in your chart. Remember to include any snacks, such as chips or fruit, that you eat between mealtimes.

Weekly food intake

Day/time	Carbos	Proteins	Vitamins	Fats
Monday 7 A.M.	Toast	Eggs	Orange juice	Butter
10.45 A.M.	Chips			
12.30 P.M.	Rice	Chicken	Salad Apple	
4 P.M.	Bread			Peanut butter

3 Check your chart each day. For a balanced diet, you should have entries in each column. The more energy you use, the more carbohydrates and fats you need to eat.

IMPROVING FARMING

● To improve and vary crops, scientists cross one successful crop plant with another to produce a new plant, called a hybrid, that has the best qualities of both plants.

● Over the last 100 years, wider use of machinery and intensive research into seeds, pest control, and soil have greatly improved food production. But farmers with no money and poor growing conditions still struggle. Scientists continue to develop drought-resistant and disease-resistant seeds to help reduce famine in developing countries.

● Genetically modified (GM) crops are now being developed and tested. They may reduce the need for pesticides and some already give high crop yields (production).

● Hydroponics is a method of growing crops without soil. It is especially useful for testing what conditions plants need to grow best. The plant roots are immersed in a mixture of water, nutrients, and sand or gravel.

Nutrient solution

FARMING FACTS AND FIGURES

Humans have adapted about half the land on Earth's surface into towns, cities, and farming land (including crop fields and pasture).

Food production

● China grows the most crops in the world—about 19 percent of total production.

● The U.S.A. produces 14 percent of the world's crops.

● America and Europe together produce enough grain to feed everyone in the world.

● In 1850, each U.S. farmer produced, on average, enough food to feed 5 people. Now, each farmer can produce enough for 78 people.

Farming disasters

● Crop farmers dislike locusts because they have a huge appetite. One locust can eat its own weight in food every day.

Locust

● A swarm of locusts can contain one billion insects. One swarm can eat 20,000 tons of plants in a day.

● In the 1800s, a potato famine killed one-fifth of the population of Ireland. At this time, many Irish people emigrated (moved away) to America.

Fascinating facts

● The word "banana" comes from *banan*, the Arabic word for "finger."

● Bananas first arrived in the U.S.A. in 1876.

● Most of the world's cocoa is produced in the Ivory Coast, in Africa.

● Ice cream cones were first served at the St. Louis World's Fair in 1904. A thin, crisp waffle was rolled into a handy holder for a scoop of ice cream.

● The first successful gasoline-driven tractors were made in the U.S.A. in the early 1890s.

● Oranges look shiny in markets because they are often coated with wax or oil to keep them from spoiling.

● Native Americans introduced Europeans to avocados, chocolate, corn, peanuts, peppers, and tomatoes.

GLOSSARY

arable farming
Crop farming.

cash crops
Crops that are grown especially to be sold in other countries.

cereal crops
Types of grass, such as wheat or corn, that produce an edible grain.

climate
The average weather an area has over the year.

developed countries
Countries where there are lots of industries and most people have a good standard of living.

developing countries
Countries where there are few industries and many people live in poverty.

food web
The way in which living things in a habitat rely on each other for food.

habitat
A place where a plant or animal lives.

herbivore
Animal that eats plants.

intensive farming
A modern farming practice that uses machinery on large farms to produce large crops cheaply.

livestock
Animals that are farmed.

mixed farming
Farming that combines rearing livestock with growing crops.

monoculture
An area in which only one main crop is grown.

organic farming
Producing crops without using chemical pesticides or fertilizers.

plantation
A monoculture farm, especially in tropical countries, where cash crops are grown on a large scale.

slash-and-burn
A farming practice where areas of tropical forest are cleared to grow crops until soil is exhausted. Also called shifting agriculture.

staple diet
The most common food eaten by people in a region or country.

subsistence farming
Small-scale farming, where farmers only grow enough to feed one family.

sustainable farming
Looking after soil and the environment so that the same land can be farmed year after year.

temperate regions
The parts of the world where temperatures are moderate, and where there is often a marked difference between the seasons.

tropical regions
The parts of the world, near the equator, where the climate is hot all year round. Tropical regions have a wet season and a dry season.

INDEX

PICTURE CREDITS

Abbreviations: t-top, m-middle, b-bottom, r-right, l-left, c-center.
All photographs supplied by Select Pictures, except for 5tl, 10mr, 13t—Stockbyte. 8mr, 16c—John Deere. 11br—Corbis/Royalty Free. 20tl—Galen Rowell/CORBIS. 22ml—Chris Mattison/FLPA-Images of Nature.